EDGE BOOKS

THE SCIENCE BEHIND
NATURAL PHENOMENA

THE SCIENCE BEHIND

WONDERS OF
EARTH

CAVE CRYSTALS, BALANCING ROCKS AND SNOW DOUGHNUTS

BY AMIE JANE LEAVITT

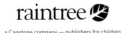

raintree
a Capstone company — publishers for children

Raintree is an imprint of Capstone Global Library Limited, a company incorporated in England and Wales having its registered office at 264 Banbury Road, Oxford, OX2 7DY – Registered company number: 6695582

www.raintree.co.uk
myorders@raintree.co.uk

ISBN 978 1 4747 2165 3 (hardback)
20 19 18 17 16
10 9 8 7 6 5 4 3 2 1

ISBN 978 1 4747 2169 1 (paperback)
21 20 19 18 17
10 9 8 7 6 5 4 3 2 1

British Library Cataloguing in Publication Data
A full catalogue record for this book is available from the British Library.

Editorial Credits
Linda Staniford, editor; Terri Poburka, designer;
Svetlana Zhurkin, media researcher; Katy LaVigne, production specialist

Photo Credits
Alamy: Tom Uhlman, 7; Corbis: George Steinmetz, 28–29; Dreamstime: David Hughes, 21, Trevor Allen, 21 (inset); iStockphoto: FransTD, 16–17; National Geographic Creative: Speleoresearch & Films/Carsten Peter, 18; Newscom: Universal Images Group/DEA/C. Sappa, 24, Westend61 GmbH/Walter G. Allgöwer, 8; Shutterstock: Aleksey Sagitov, 17 (top right), Alexey Kljatov, 19, chris64, 25 (top), EcoPrint, 14, Filip Fuxa, 24–25, KPG Idream, 22 (bottom), Leonard Zhukovsky, 23, Nagel Photography, cover, Natalia Bratslavsky, 11, Photovolcanica, 15, Tami Freed, 27, Timothy Hodgkinson, 5, underworld, 22 (top), Vadym Zaitsev, 14–15, VikaSuh, 1 and throughout, Zack Frank, 17 (top left); SuperStock: age fotostock/Cody Duncan, 12

We would like to thank Dr Sandra Mather, Professor Emerita, Department of Geology and Astronomy, West Chester University, West Chester, Pennsylvania, USA, for her invaluable help in the preparation of this book.

Every effort has been made to contact copyright holders of material reproduced in this book. Any omissions will be rectified in subsequent printings if notice is given to the publisher.

All the Internet addresses (URLs) given in this book were valid at the time of going to press. However, due to the dynamic nature of the Internet, some addresses may have changed, or sites may have changed or ceased to exist since publication. While the author and publisher regret any inconvenience this may cause readers, no responsibility for any such changes can be accepted by either the author or the publisher.

Printed and bound in China.

CONTENTS

THE WONDERS OF EARTH

From space, Earth looks like a giant blue marble. It has swirling white frothy clouds, emerald-green and chocolate-brown landscapes, and huge sapphire oceans. From this vantage point high above Earth, everything looks smooth. It's only the colour that distinguishes one area from another. However, when you zoom in and look at Earth closely, you discover that the planet has all kinds of different **topographical** features. If you take an even closer look, you'll discover that every part of the planet has its own unique phenomena.

What causes the physical landscape of Earth to have such diversity? This question and others like it have intrigued humans for a long time. For thousands of years, people made up stories to explain the strange things they saw on Earth. Today science provides the explanations for many of these natural phenomena.

topographical relating to the physical
features of an area of Earth

SNOW DOUGHNUTS

On a snowy day in 2007, road maintenance crews in Washington, USA, spotted something unusual on the road. There, out in the snow, was an object that looked like a giant tyre covered in snow. This unusual feature wasn't a tyre, though. It wasn't made by humans, either. It was a natural formation called a snow doughnut.

Mike Stanford, an employee of the Washington State Department of Transportation, was one of the men on the crew. He had worked as an **avalanche forecaster** for more than 30 years. Because of that, he often saw unusual snow features. But he told news reporters that this was the biggest snow doughnut he had ever seen. It measured 66 centimetres (26 inches) tall. The centre hole was 20 centimetres (8 inches) in diameter.

avalanche forecaster person who predicts where and when avalanches, or snowslides, will occur

Snow doughnuts are made from very loosely packed snow, so the snow in the middle of the roll can be blown away by the wind, making a hole.

Snow doughnuts are rare. That's because snow doughnuts need special weather conditions to form:

1. The ground must be covered with a layer of icy, crusty snow. This prevents freshly fallen snow from sticking to it.

2. There must be a blanket of 2.5 to 5 centimetres (1 to 2 inches) of wet, new snow on top of the icy, crusty snow.

3. A force needs to move the freshly fallen snow. It can either be a strong, steady wind or **gravity**. The wind causes the snow blanket to roll into the doughnut shape, picking up more snow as it moves. On an incline, gravity helps to pull the doughnut down the slope. The centre of the snow doughnut will be hollow. That's because the snow in the centre will either be blown out by the wind or will collapse as the tube rolls along.

gravity force that pulls objects with mass together; gravity pulls objects towards the centre of Earth

SLIDING STONES

Death Valley Desert in California, USA, is a special place. It is home to North America's lowest point, Badwater Basin, which is 86 metres (282 feet) below sea level. But this isn't the only feature that makes Death Valley unusual. This region is also home to the famous sliding stones of Racetrack Playa.

When people come to Racetrack Playa, they immediately notice the huge boulders scattered across the ground. These boulders have trails extending behind them. Some trails are long and straight. Others curve and snake across the dry lakebed.

The trails show that the boulders have moved. But how? What moved them? Some are as big as 272 kilograms (600 pounds). They certainly cannot be moved easily. The lakebed is flat, so gravity didn't move them. Because of the boulders' enormous size, wind wouldn't easily be able to push them across the dry soil. There's too much **friction** for that. There are no footprints, car tyre marks or other tracks found near the trails, so it's unlikely that a person moved them.

friction force produced when two objects rub against each other; friction slows moving objects

AMAZING FACT

Playa is a Spanish word. It means "beach" or "dry lakebed".

When it rains in Death Valley, a shallow lake forms on the surface of the dry valley. It freezes at night into a thin sheet of ice.

Scientists searched for answers for decades. In 2004 a team of scientists finally solved the Racetrack Playa mystery. Here's what they found:

1. It doesn't rain very often in Death Valley, but when it does, the rain covers the dry lakebed in a thin sheet of water. Very little water seeps into the soil.

2. When the sun sets, the temperature in the desert drops drastically. The thin layer of water on the lakebed freezes.

3. In the morning, the ice starts to melt. When it does, the ice sheet crackles and snaps into thin pieces.

4. Then, when conditions are right, the wind starts to blow. The wind pushes the ice up against the boulders. The ice acts like a sail on a ship. It catches the wind and pushes the rocks forward like a ship on the water. The rocks don't move quickly. They creep along the surface. As they move, they dig into the muddy lakebed and leave a trail behind them.

5. The sun's rays continue to heat up the desert floor until the ice has melted and the water has **evaporated**. Then the rocks stop moving.

evaporate change from a liquid to a gas

CAVES

Caves come in all different shapes and sizes. Some are just small holes in the ground, barely big enough for a person to squeeze inside. Others are so huge that an entire army can fit inside! The "Chapel Room" in Organ Cave, West Virginia, USA, was used during the American Civil War (1861–1865). Approximately 1,100 soldiers held weekly Sunday worship services inside the cave.

Caves form in three main ways:

1. **Rainwater** Rain falls from the sky. It seeps into the soil. The water picks up **carbon dioxide** from decaying plants. The water and carbon dioxide combine to make carbonic acid. Acid breaks down certain rocks.

Rainwater and carbon dioxide formed these cave formations in the Cango Caves, South Africa.

When the carbonic acid passes through limestone, it dissolves the limestone. The holes left in the limestone eventually form a cave.

2. **Waves** Ocean and lake waves crash onto the shore. The water and rock particles wear away the rocks. Over time, more and more of the rocks along the shore wear away. A cave is formed.

Waves wear away rock over time to form sea caves. ←

3. **Lava** Lava is **molten** rock. It flows from volcanoes. In the middle of a lava flow is a channel. The lava moves most quickly inside the channel. The slower-moving lava is on the outside of the channel. Lava on the edges of the channel cools first. If the lava on the top of the flow cools but the lava inside the channel keeps flowing, then a tube is formed. When the flow cools, a cave is formed. Sometimes the roof of the tube collapses over time, making another kind of entrance to the cave.

When this lava has cooled, it may form a lava tube.

carbon dioxide colourless, odourless gas that people and animals breathe out

molten liquid or melted

There are many interesting caves around the world.
Here are three of them:

Mammoth Cave in Kentucky, USA, was formed by rainwater.
It is the world's longest known cave system. More than
587 kilometres (365 miles) of the cave network have already
been explored. And there's still more to go!

New Zealand's **Rikoriko Cave** is one of the largest sea caves
in the world. It is so large that tour boats 80 metres (60 feet)
long can easily fit inside.

Jeju Volcanic Island and Lava Tubes are found in South Korea.
In the lava tubes, the walls are multicoloured orange, white
and brown. **Stalagmites** and **stalactites** extend from the floor
and ceiling. Over the years, water has continued to drip in
the cave and has formed these structures by leaving minerals
such as calcium behind.

The Manjanggul Lava Tube Cave on Jeju Volcanic Island in
South Korea is 7.4 kilometres (4.6 miles) long.

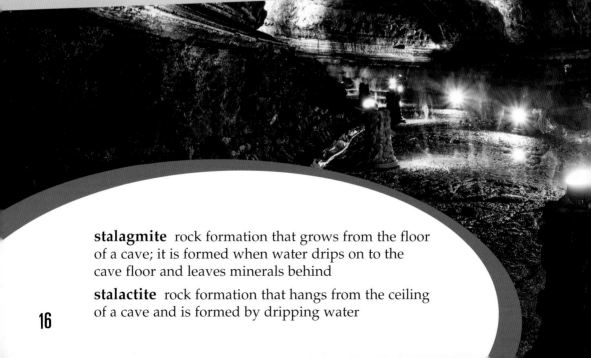

stalagmite rock formation that grows from the floor
of a cave; it is formed when water drips on to the
cave floor and leaves minerals behind

stalactite rock formation that hangs from the ceiling
of a cave and is formed by dripping water

Many different formations can be seen in this cave.

Cave formations

Stalagmites and stalactites are just two of the different types of formation made by water dripping in limestone caves. Stalagmites are usually found directly below stalactites. They can even join to form pillars or columns.

Other formations include:

- Straws – thin-walled hollow formations like drinking straws

- Shawls or curtains – when water trickles down a rock face, it can deposit minerals that form a thin sheet growing at an angle from the rock face. The sheet can sometimes have folds in it like fabric, and it may have different-coloured bands caused by different minerals.

- Flowstones – formed when water flows over the floor of a cave

- Helictites – formed when water comes into the cave through cracks in the stone. The mineral deposits grow into small delicate formations like ribbons or threads.

GIANT CRYSTALS

In April 2000 two brothers in Mexico found a very special cave 305 metres (1,000 feet) below a lead and silver mine. This cave is different from most other caves. Most caves are chilly, but this cave is hot. It's about 44 degrees Celsius (112 degrees Fahrenheit). The reason for the extreme temperature is the cave's location. It is located directly over **magma.**

The hot, moist conditions of the cave provide the perfect setting for the growth of **crystals** – and not just small sparklers. These crystals are huge! Some of the crystals in this cave are 9 metres (30 feet) long and about a metre thick. These **translucent** crystals, which are made of the mineral selenite, are also soft. You can easily scratch or damage them.

What are crystals?

Crystals are minerals that have formed into a particular shape. They often have flat sides and can form regular shapes. The shapes they make depend on the molecules and atoms that make up the crystal. Salt and snowflakes are types of crystals. Precious stones such as diamonds are also crystals. The crystals in the Cave of Crystals in Mexico are made of selenite, which is a form of the common mineral gypsum. Gypsum is a soft mineral used in plaster, fertilizer and blackboard chalk.

Snowflakes are a type of crystal. Each one is different.

The crystals formed over hundreds of thousands of years. Groundwater filled with minerals came into the cave. The hot, moist conditions of the cave caused the atoms that make up the minerals to attach to each other. Over time, the crystals grew larger and larger.

magma molten rock below the surface of Earth

crystal mineral that has formed into a particular shape

translucent allowing some light to pass through

BASALT COLUMNS

Basalt columns are made out of a volcanic rock called **basalt**. These special columns formed millions of years ago when volcanoes erupted and lava flowed across Earth's surface. When the flow cooled, lava in the interior of the flow cooled more slowly than the exterior. This allowed the columnar jointing to form. These tall columns have five, six or seven sides.

Basalt columns are found in many places on Earth. Here are some of the most famous:

Giant's Causeway, Northern Ireland — Forty thousand interlocking basalt columns rise above the ocean in cliffs 100 metres (330 feet) tall. Each column is 38 to 51 centimetres (15 to 20 inches) in diameter.

Devils Tower, Wyoming, USA — This huge rock formation juts out of the flat Wyoming plains. It is made up of thousands of basalt columns.

Hexagon Pool, Golan Heights, Israel — Six-sided basalt columns surround a giant pool which is fed by the Hexagon River.

AMAZING FACT

Basalt columns aren't just limited to Earth. In 2008 the Mars Reconnaissance Orbiter (MRO) found basalt columns on Mars.

basalt hard, dark rock made from cooled lava

Giant's Causeway in Northern Ireland is made up of thousands of interlocking basalt columns.

Balancing Rock

In Nova Scotia, Canada, there is a rock formation called Balancing Rock. It is a tall basalt column that stands all alone and looks like it could topple over at any minute! This rock was formed as the basalt columns around it wore away over hundreds of thousands of years. Eventually this rock will fall away too.

EROSIONAL LANDFORMS

Arches, bridges, stacks, stumps and sea caves all have one thing in common: they result from long-term **erosion** by wind and water. Wind blasts the rock layers with small pieces of rock. Water carrying rocks and shells crashes into rock layers and slowly wears them away. Rainwater combines with carbon dioxide in the air to form carbonic acid, which erodes rock. Water collects in cracks in the rock and expands as it freezes, opening the cracks wider and **weathering** the rock.

Erosional landforms occur along coastlines where seawater crashes onto the shore. They also occur in deserts. Geologists believe that the desert landforms are a result of both wind and water erosion and weathering. Water in the desert comes from rainwater, flash floods and frosts.

arch

COASTLINE EROSIONAL LANDFORMS

Arch: Crashing waves work on both sides of a rock jutting into the water.

Stack: Water erodes soft rock below a layer of hard rock. Stacks can also form when water erodes the rock at water level. A stack might also be the remnants of an arch that has eroded away.

stack

Stump: When a stack has worn away, it collapses to form a stump.

hoodoo

DESERT EROSIONAL LANDFORMS

Stack: Wind erodes a softer layer of rock that is found underneath a stronger layer of rock that resists the wind.

Bridge: Streams that have long ago dried up eroded soft rock beneath a layer of harder rock to form some bridges. Others are formed by weathering.

Hoodoo: Frost weathering and erosion from rainwater are both responsible for the formation of hoodoos. These tall, thin spires of rock often have strange shapes.

Slot Canyon: Water flows into a hairline crack in the sandstone and erodes the rock, forming a narrow canyon. The canyon gets deeper and wider over time until a slot canyon is formed.

erosion mechanical breaking down of material by wind or water

weathering action of weather conditions in changing the colour, texture and form of exposed materials, such as rock

Delicate Arch in Utah, USA, is 20 metres (65 feet) tall.

Erosional landforms are found all over the world. Here are some of the most famous:

Arches National Park in Utah, USA, has the largest collection of natural arches in the world. There are more than 2,000 arches in the park. The area also has a wide selection of bridges, pillars and other formations created by the erosion of sandstone and other sedimentary rock.

Fairy Bridge in China, the world's largest documented natural bridge, is 122 metres (400 feet) wide. Water carved the bridge by slowly dissolving layers of limestone.

Aloba Arch in Chad is one of the world's tallest arches. It measures 120 metres (394 feet) tall and 76 metres (250 feet) wide. It is located in the Sahara Desert.

Aloba Arch, Chad

Durdle Door, UK

Durdle Door is one of the most famous rock formations in the UK. It was formed when the sea punched through a layer of soft rock, leaving an arch of hard limestone behind. The name "Durdle" comes from an old English word meaning bore or drill. Other sea arches can be found in Cabo San Lucas in Mexico, Es Pontás in Mallorca and Hopewell Rocks in Canada.

SINKHOLES

Sinkholes form in areas where there are limestone and other carbonate rocks. That's because this type of rock dissolves constantly. Some sinkholes form below Earth's surface. Other sinkholes form on top of Earth's surface. Sinkholes are found all around the world.

Here are some of the most famous sinkholes:

The **Great Blue Hole**, a famous sinkhole in Belize, Central America, measures 305 metres (1,000 feet) wide and 122 metres (400 feet) deep. Originally a cave on land, the cave filled with seawater when the sea level rose. Scuba divers enjoy exploring the Great Blue Hole.

carbonate sedimentary rocks made up of carbonite minerals such as calcite or aragonite

The Great Blue Hole in the Caribbean Ocean is a famous diving spot.

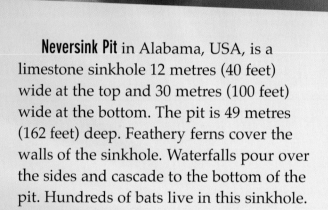

Neversink Pit in Alabama, USA, is a limestone sinkhole 12 metres (40 feet) wide at the top and 30 metres (100 feet) wide at the bottom. The pit is 49 metres (162 feet) deep. Feathery ferns cover the walls of the sinkhole. Waterfalls pour over the sides and cascade to the bottom of the pit. Hundreds of bats live in this sinkhole.

High desert cliffs surround **Numby Numby**, a sinkhole in Australia. Natural springs fill the sinkhole with water at a constant temperature of 32°C (90°F).

Earth is indeed a fascinating place, but we still have a lot more to learn about it. As we embark on more journeys of discovery, who knows what new landforms and other wonders we'll find. Only time, observation and scientific research will tell!

Cave explorers use ropes to explore Neversink Pit. →

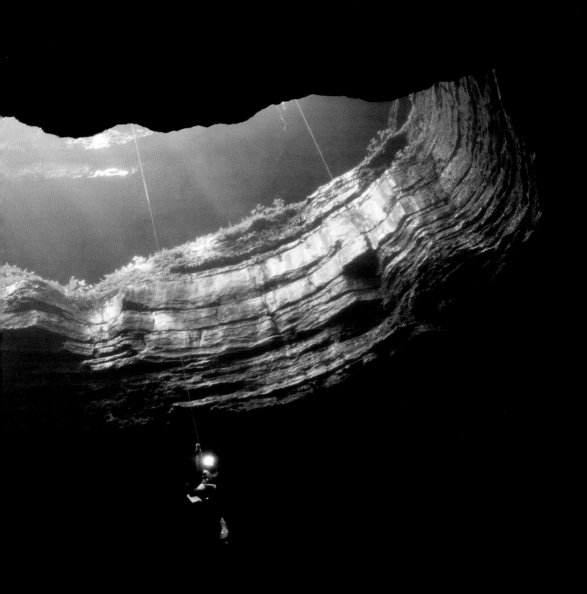

Glossary

avalanche forecaster person who predicts where and when avalanches, or snowslides, will occur

basalt hard, dark rock made from cooled lava

carbonate sedimentary rocks made up of carbonite minerals such as calcite or aragonite

carbon dioxide colourless, odourless gas that people and animals breathe out

crystal mineral that has formed into a particular shape

erosion mechanical breaking down of material by wind or water

evaporate change from a liquid to a gas

friction force produced when two objects rub against each other; friction slows moving objects

gravity force that pulls objects with mass together; gravity pulls objects towards the centre of Earth

magma molten rock beneath the surface of Earth

molten liquid or melted

stalactite rock formation that hangs from the ceiling of a cave and is formed by dripping water

stalagmite rock formation that grows from the floor of a cave; it is formed when water drips onto the cave floor and leaves minerals behind

topographical relating to the physical features of an area of Earth

translucent allowing some light to pass through

weathering action of weather conditions in changing the colour, texture and form of exposed materials, such as rock

Find out more

Books

Caves (Explorer Travel Guides), Anna Claybourne (Raintree, 2013)

Rocks (Earth Cycles), Jillian Powell (Franklin Watts, 2014)

The Usborne Encyclopedia of Planet Earth, Anna Claybourne and Gill Doherty (Usborne, 2013)

Websites

www.dkfindout.com/uk/earth
Learn more about Earth's landforms.

www.onegeology.org/extra/kids/earthProcesses/home.html
Discover more about how natural forces change Earth.

Comprehension questions

1. Explain how stalagmites are formed.
2. How does weathering cause an arch to form in rock in a desert?
3. Describe the weather conditions needed for snow doughnuts to form.

Index